THE BEST NFL
RECEIVERS
OF ALL TIME

By Barry Wilner

Published by ABDO Publishing Company, PO Box 398166, Minneapolis, MN 55439. Copyright © 2014 by Abdo Consulting Group, Inc. International copyrights reserved in all countries. No part of this book may be reproduced in any form without written permission from the publisher. SportsZone™ is a trademark and logo of ABDO Publishing Company.

Printed in the United States of America, North Mankato, Minnesota
052013
012014

Editor: Chrös McDougall
Series Designer: Christa Schneider

Photo Credits: Mark Brettingen/AP Images, cover (left), 1 (left); Rick Osentoski/AP Images, cover (right), 1 (right), 61; AP Images, 7, 11, 17, 21; Robert Walsh/AP Images, 9; NFL Photos/AP Images, 13, 19; Pro Football Hall of Fame via AP Images, 15; Tom Reed/AP Images, 23; Gary Stewart/AP Images, 25; Tannen Maury/AP Images, 27; Martha Jane Stanton/AP Images, 29; Tom Olmscheid/AP Images, 31, 33; Scott Boehm/AP Images, 35; G. Newman Lowrance/AP Images, 37, 41; Al Golub/AP Images, 39; Paul Spinelli/AP Images, 43; Brian Garfinkel/AP Images, 45; John Bazemore/AP Images, 47; Evan Pinkus/AP Images, 49; Kevin Terrell/AP Images, 51; Darron Cummings/AP Images, 53; Mark J. Terrill/AP Images, 55; Paul Connors/AP Images, 57; Carlos Osorio/AP Images, 59

Library of Congress Control Number: 2013931964

Cataloging-in-Publication Data
Wilner, Barry.
 The best NFL receivers of all time / Barry Wilner.
   p. cm. -- (NFL's best ever)
Includes bibliographical references and index.
ISBN 978-1-61783-911-5
1. National Football League--Juvenile literature. 2. Wide receivers (Football)--Juvenile literature.   I. Title.
796.332--dc23

                                        2013931964

TABLE OF CONTENTS

Introduction   4

Don Hutson   6

Raymond Berry   10

Lance Alworth   14

Paul Warfield   18

Steve Largent   22

Jerry Rice   26

Cris Carter   30

Marvin Harrison   34

Terrell Owens   38

Tony Gonzalez   42

Randy Moss   46

Reggie Wayne   50

Larry Fitzgerald   54

Calvin Johnson   58

Honorable Mentions   62

Glossary   63

For More Information   63

Index   64

About the Author   64

INTRODUCTION

Baseball has the home run. Basketball has the slam dunk. For football, the most exciting play is the long touchdown pass.

It happens in an instant. But there is nothing like a wide receiver sprinting down the field and catching a perfectly thrown ball while in stride.

Some of the best receivers in National Football League (NFL) history specialized in catching deep balls. Others excelled on slants and screens, post patterns, or stop-and-go routes. Some were extremely fast. Some were extremely shifty. Others stood out for their strength or smarts. And the best of the best could do it all.

Here are some of the best receivers in NFL history.

DON
HUTSON

At a time when few NFL teams passed the ball, Don Hutson caught seemingly everything thrown to him. And when he caught a ball, he was so quick that he was hard to take down. Hutson showed his speed in just his second game in the league. The Green Bay Packers receiver caught a ball. Then he sped 83 yards down the field for a touchdown. Such was life for the NFL's first great wide receiver.

"In the era he played in, he was the dominant player in the game," said former Green Bay general manager Ron Wolf. "Not just as a receiver, but as a kicker and with his ability to play defense."

Don Hutson was a star wide receiver for the Green Bay Packers in an era before passing was common.

That's right. Hutson was a safety and a kicker for the Packers, too. It was at receiver where he truly shined, though.

Hutson was known in college at the University of Alabama as the "Alabama Antelope" because he ran so smoothly. That led to a lot of touchdowns in the NFL. He caught 99 touchdown passes in his pro career. That stood as a record until Steve Largent broke it in 1989.

Hutson was a key player on Packers teams that won three NFL championships (the Super Bowl did not begin until after the 1966 season). He was twice the NFL's Most Valuable Player (MVP), in 1941 and 1942. He led the NFL in receiving eight times. And 50 years after he retired, he still held some league records. It was no wonder that Hutson was named to the first class of the Pro Football Hall of Fame in 1963.

29

The number of points Hutson scored in one quarter against the Detroit Lions in a 1945 game.

Don Hutson of the Green Bay Packers was in a league of his own as a wide receiver during the 1930s and 1940s.

DON HUTSON

Hometown: Pine Bluff, Arkansas

College: University of Alabama

Height, Weight: 6-foot-1, 183 pounds

Birth Date: January 31, 1913

Team: Green Bay Packers (1935–45)

All-Pro: 1938, 1939, 1940, 1941, 1942, 1943, 1944, 1945

Pro Bowls: 1939, 1940, 1941, 1942

RAYMOND BERRY

Some say Raymond Berry was the best receiver at running pass routes.
Berry himself once said he had 88 different moves he could use to get open. And he mastered those moves despite having one leg shorter than the other.

Berry wore special shoes to play. It didn't hurt that he also had great hands. Johnny Unitas was Berry's quarterback with two Baltimore Colts championship teams. Unitas once said he never saw Berry drop a ball, not in a game or even in practice. In fact, in his 13 pro seasons Berry only fumbled once.

Berry certainly didn't make any mistakes in the most famous game in NFL history. The Colts played the New York Giants for the 1958 championship. It was broadcast nationally. And it became known for its exciting finish.

Raymond Berry was a key player in the Baltimore Colts' great offenses in the 1950s and 1960s.

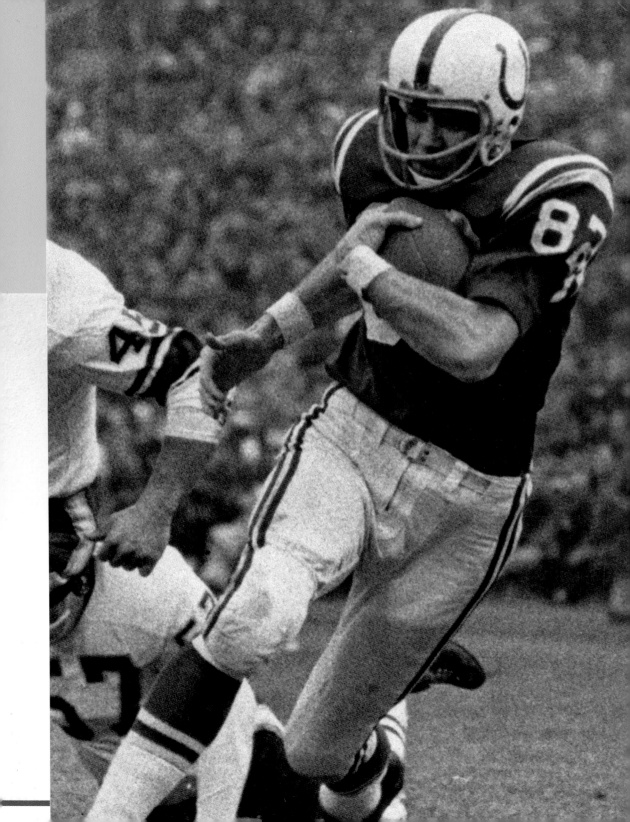

Baltimore was trailing by three points and needed a last-minute scoring drive. So Unitas kept throwing to Berry. And Berry kept catching the ball. The Colts eventually kicked a field goal to tie the score. It became the first title game to go into overtime.

Once there, Berry picked up 33 yards on two receptions. His Colts soon scored the winning touchdown. Berry set a record with 12 catches in the game. He had 178 yards and a touchdown.

By the end of his career, Berry had a then-record 631 catches for 9,275 yards and 68 touchdowns. He led the league in catches in 1958, 1959, and 1960. And in 1973, he was elected into the Hall of Fame.

1,298

The number of receiving yards Berry gained in 1960, the most in NFL history to that point. He did it on 74 catches.

Raymond Berry of the Baltimore Colts snags a pass during a 1966 game against the Los Angeles Rams.

RAYMOND BERRY

Hometown: Corpus Christi, Texas

College: Southern Methodist University

Height, Weight: 6-foot-2, 187 pounds

Birth Date: February 27, 1933

Team: Baltimore Colts (1955–67)

All-Pro: 1958, 1959, 1960

Pro Bowls: 1958, 1959, 1960, 1961, 1963, 1964

LANCE ALWORTH

Lance Alworth's nickname was "Bambi." He was as graceful as a deer running through a forest—maybe just as fast, too. Alworth was a great running back at the University of Arkansas. He also was a smart student. He made the academic All-America team three times.

Alworth began his pro career with the San Diego Chargers, who converted him to a receiver, in 1962. The Chargers were in the rival American Football League (AFL) at the time. It was a big deal for the AFL to sign such a good player. And Alworth quickly became the AFL's best pass catcher.

"You could see right from the start that he was going to be a superstar," said Oakland Raiders owner Al Davis. Davis was the scout who originally signed Alworth to the Chargers.

Lance Alworth made his name as a receiver for the San Diego Chargers in the upstart AFL.

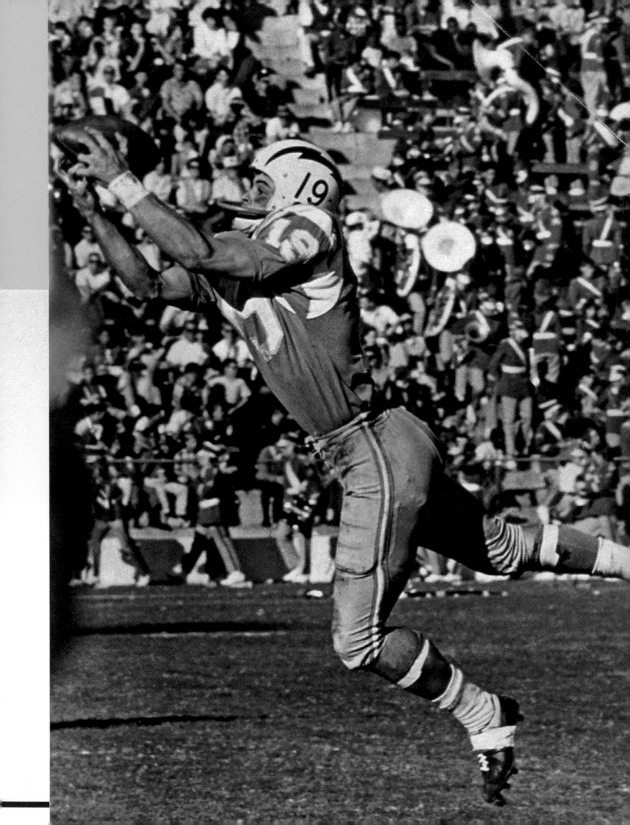

When No. 19 broke free over the middle or deep down the field, it usually meant a touchdown. Alworth scored 85 receiving touchdowns. On many of those touchdowns, he never was touched. That is because he had great timing. Alworth often jumped over taller defenders to catch the ball. When he landed, he took off like, well, a deer. That is how he scored on a 48-yard play in the Chargers' 1963 AFL championship game victory.

Alworth won another championship after the AFL and NFL merged in 1970. This time he was playing for the Dallas Cowboys. But his legacy remains in the AFL. In 1978, Alworth became the very first AFL player elected to the Pro Football Hall of Fame.

40

The number of receiving touchdowns Alworth scored in 1964, 1965, and 1966 combined. He led the AFL in scores each year (13, 14, and 13).

The San Diego Chargers' Lance Alworth reaches to catch a pass during a 1963 photo shoot.

LANCE ALWORTH

Hometown: Houston, Texas

College: University of Arkansas

Height, Weight: 6-foot, 184 pounds

Birth Date: August 3, 1940

Teams: San Diego Chargers (1962–70)
Dallas Cowboys (1971–72)

All-Pro: 1963, 1964, 1965, 1966, 1967, 1968

AFL All-Star Games: 1963, 1964, 1965, 1966, 1967, 1968, 1969

Super Bowl: VI

PAUL WARFIELD

The 1963 Cleveland Browns went 10–4 on the season as a run-first team. After all, they featured one of the greatest running backs ever in Jim Brown. So some were surprised by their first-round pick in the 1964 NFL Draft. The Browns selected wide receiver Paul Warfield.

One look at how Warfield could run past defenders, though, and anyone could tell why. The Browns quickly showed they knew what they were doing. Cleveland won the NFL championship that season.

Warfield was so dangerous on deep passes that many defenses put two players on him. Double-teaming was unusual in those days. And it made the Browns tougher to handle. Brown, after all, could run over, around, and through tacklers. And Warfield could fly past them.

Paul Warfield combined with star running back Jim Brown to give the Cleveland Browns a top offense.

The Browns traded Warfield to the Miami Dolphins in 1970. The Dolphins were another run-first team. But Warfield's speed, strength, and jumping skills made coach Don Shula think more about throwing the ball. Warfield had a league-high 11 touchdown catches in 1971. Two years later, he again scored 11 times. Meanwhile, the Dolphins won their second consecutive Super Bowl after the 1973 season.

Warfield left Miami for an upstart pro league in 1975. But Warfield was back in the NFL and back with the Browns the next year. Playing on run-first teams affected Warfield's stats. Still, he averaged 20.1 yards per catch over his career. Plus he added 85 touchdowns. That helped him earn his spot in the Hall of Fame in 1983.

17

The number of wins by the 1972 Miami Dolphins, out of 17 games. Through 2012, the 1972 Dolphins remain the only team to go undefeated and win a Super Bowl.

Paul Warfield of the Miami Dolphins side steps a Houston Oilers defender during a 1970 game.

PAUL WARFIELD

Hometown: Warren, Ohio

College: Ohio State University

Height, Weight: 6-foot, 188 pounds

Birth Date: November 28, 1942

Teams: Cleveland Browns (1964–69, 1976–77)
  Miami Dolphins (1970–74)

All-Pro: 1971, 1973

Pro Bowls: 1964, 1968, 1969, 1970, 1971, 1972, 1973, 1974

Super Bowls: VI, VII, VIII

STEVE
LARGENT

The Houston Oilers made a big mistake when they decided that Steve Largent was too small and too slow for pro football. Houston couldn't find room for the rookie after four exhibition games. So it traded him to a brand new NFL team starting out in Seattle.

In need of players, the Seattle Seahawks took a chance on Largent. He paid them back with one of the greatest careers in NFL history.

By his third season, Largent was making the Pro Bowl. By his fourth, he was leading the league in receiving yards with 1,237.

Largent also was a leader on and off the field. Usually new teams struggle for several seasons. But the Seahawks had a winning 9–7 record by just their third season.

The Seattle Seahawks' Steve Largent proved that smaller wide receivers could have a great impact in the NFL.

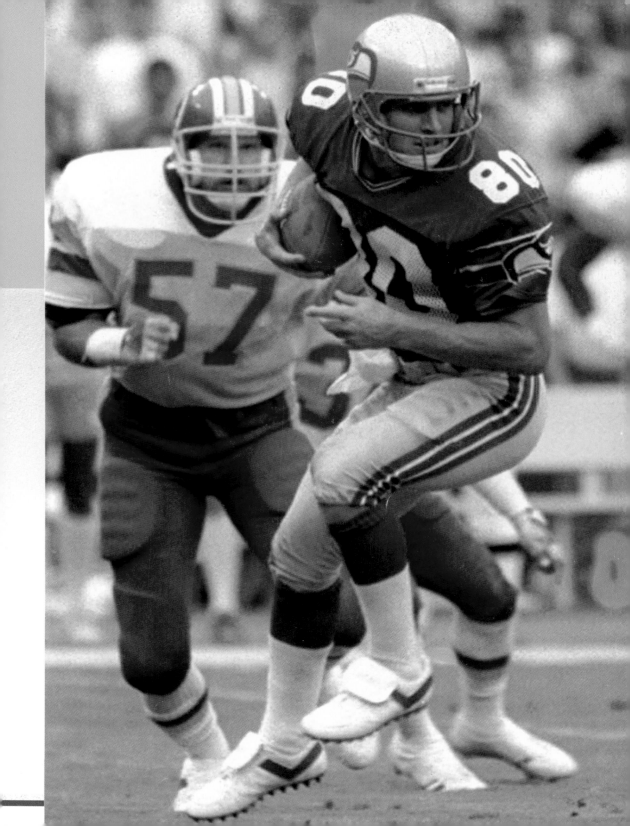

Largent has joked that the Oilers were right. He was too slow and small for anyone to expect him to be a star. But he always played hard and smart, and he kept a winning outlook.

Largent played all 14 of his NFL seasons in Seattle. When he retired, he held six major career receiving records. Among them were most catches (819), most games in a row with a catch (177), most touchdown catches (100), and most yards on receptions (13,089).

"If you're a Seahawk, you know who Steve Largent is," said Seattle defensive end Red Bryant in 2012.

After football, Largent found another rewarding career in politics. He served as a US representative from his home state of Oklahoma from 1994 to 2002.

177

The record number of consecutive games in which Largent caught a pass in his Hall of Fame career. Ark Monk and Jerry Rice have since broken it.

Steve Largent of the Seattle Seahawks heads to the end zone against the Minnesota Vikings in 1986.

STEVE LARGENT

Hometown: Tulsa, Oklahoma

College: University of Tulsa

Height, Weight: 5-foot-11, 187 pounds

Birth Date: September 28, 1954

Team: Seattle Seahawks (1976–89)

All-Pro: 1985

Pro Bowls: 1978, 1979, 1981, 1984, 1985, 1986, 1987

JERRY RICE

Jerry Rice saw "The Hill" as an opponent. He believed that if he could beat "The Hill," which was a 2.5-mile uphill run, that he could be ready for anything on the football field.

"The training I used to do in the offseason helped make me the great player that I was," said Rice, the NFL's record holder in nearly every receiving category.

That extra edge turned Rice into arguably the most dangerous pass catcher the game has seen. He caught 1,549 passes in his career. That is far and away the most in NFL history. He also had 22,895 receiving yards and 197 touchdowns. Rice led the NFL in touchdown catches and receiving yards six times in his career, which was played mostly with the San Francisco 49ers.

Jerry Rice set a new standard for wide receivers during his long career, mostly with the San Francisco 49ers.

Rice had played at a small college.

He wasn't very fast or tall. And he didn't have long arms or great strength. But 49ers coach Bill Walsh saw Rice as a perfect fit for his past-happy West Coast offense.

And Walsh was right. Rice teamed with quarterbacks Joe Montana and Steve Young to win three Super Bowls during the 1980s and 1990s. He was the MVP of Super Bowl XXIII. And when he retired, he was elected into the Hall of Fame.

A players' strike in 1987 shortened his season to 12 games. Rice caught only 65 passes that season. But an amazing 22 of them were for touchdowns, which became an NFL record. Randy Moss later broke that record in a full 16-game season. But it again was proof that Rice set the standard for NFL receivers.

208

The number of touchdowns Rice scored in his career (197 receiving, 10 rushing, 1 fumble recovery return), the most of any pro player. It is 34 more than runner-up Emmitt Smith.

Jerry Rice of the San Francisco 49ers runs away from a New Orleans Saints defender for a touchdown in 1989.

JERRY RICE

Hometown: Crawford, Mississippi

College: Mississippi Valley State University

Height, Weight: 6-foot-2, 200 pounds

Birth Date: October 13, 1962

Teams: San Francisco 49ers (1985–2000)
Oakland Raiders (2001–04)
Seattle Seahawks (2004)

All-Pro: 1986, 1987, 1988, 1989, 1990, 1992, 1993, 1994, 1995, 1996

Pro Bowls: 1986, 1987, 1988, 1989, 1990, 1991, 1992, 1993, 1994, 1995, 1996, 1998, 2002

Super Bowls: XXIII, XXIV, XXIX

CRIS
CARTER

Minnesota Vikings quarterbacks learned something very quickly about Cris Carter. No matter where they threw the ball, Carter would grab it. Few if any NFL receivers have had better hands than Carter. It didn't matter if he was sprinting deep or staying short. He could always be counted on for a catch.

"I prided myself on that," Carter said. "If he was throwing to me, I was holding onto the ball."

Warren Moon was the Vikings' quarterback in 1994. Carter had 122 catches that year. That was the most in league history at the time. It also was the second of eight straight years in which Carter gained at least 1,000 yards.

Cris Carter overcame off-field adversity to become a Hall of Fame wide receiver.

Carter was known for his ability to make catches right at the edge of the field. If a pass was toward the sideline, Carter almost always came down in-bounds. He almost seemed to be tap dancing or performing ballet when he did it. Carter also was known for his near-perfect route running.

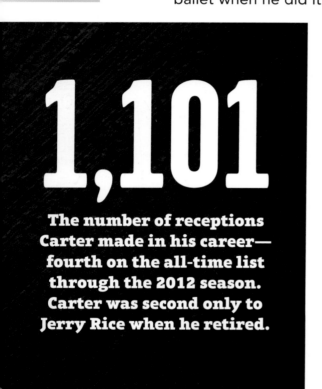

1,101

The number of receptions Carter made in his career—fourth on the all-time list through the 2012 season. Carter was second only to Jerry Rice when he retired.

Carter remained a star receiver even after Moon left the Vikings. In 1998, Minnesota went 15–1 while scoring an NFL-record 556 points. Quarterback Randall Cunningham guided the offense. He had one of the best wide receiver combinations in NFL history. Carter was on one side and rookie Randy Moss was on the other.

Carter ended up falling short of a Super Bowl in his 16 seasons. But nevertheless, he was elected to the Hall of Fame in 2013.

Cris Carter of the Minnesota Vikings runs away from a
Carolina Panthers defender in 2000.

CRIS CARTER

Hometown: Troy, Ohio

College: Ohio State University

Height, Weight: 6-foot-3, 202 pounds

Birth Date: November 25, 1965

Teams: Philadelphia Eagles (1987–89)
Minnesota Vikings (1990–2001)
Miami Dolphins (2002)

All-Pro: 1994, 1999

Pro Bowls: 1993, 1994, 1995, 1996, 1997, 1998,
1999, 2000

MARVIN HARRISON

Marvin Harrison was heading into his third season with the Indianapolis Colts when he first met quarterback Peyton Manning. They were together for the next 11 years until Harrison retired. During that time they formed perhaps the best receiver-quarterback duo in football history.

"I always knew Marvin would run the right route, catch the ball, and make a play," Manning said. "You can't ask for anyone better to throw to."

Harrison was good all over the field. He was most dangerous down the sideline, though.

Somehow he always knew how much room he had. And he seemed to find every pass, catch it, and stay inside the white sideline.

Marvin Harrison proved to be quarterback Peyton Manning's favorite target for many seasons with the Indianapolis Colts.

Harrison caught 1,102 passes in his career. That was second only to Jerry Rice when Harrison retired. In 2002, Harrison caught an amazing 143 balls. That is by far the NFL record for one season. He caught at least 100 passes for four consecutive seasons from 1999 to 2003. And for eight straight seasons, he gained at least 1,100 yards through the air. His 128 touchdown catches ranked ninth all-time through 2012.

Yet unlike many receivers, Harrison wasn't a showman. After a touchdown, he handed the football back to the officials rather than spiking it or dunking it over the goal posts. He didn't dance after scores. He didn't brag. In fact, he rarely talked. He preferred instead to focus in on his job.

965

The number of passes Harrison caught from Peyton Manning. Manning was the only starting quarterback for the Colts from 1998 until Harrison retired in 2008.

In 2007, Harrison and the Colts played in the first rainy Super Bowl. But that didn't seem to bother Harrison. He caught five passes for 59 yards and the Colts won the championship.

The Indianapolis Colts' Marvin Harrison makes a catch during a 2005 game against the San Diego Chargers.

MARVIN HARRISON

Hometown: Philadelphia, Pennsylvania

College: Syracuse University

Height, Weight: 6-foot, 175 pounds

Birth Date: August 25, 1972

Team: Indianapolis Colts (1996–2008)

All-Pro: 1999, 2002, 2006

Pro Bowls: 1999, 2000, 2001, 2002, 2003, 2004, 2005, 2006

Super Bowl: XLI

TERRELL OWENS

Only a few seconds remained in the game. The San Francisco 49ers needed a touchdown or they'd be out of the 1998 playoffs. Quarterback Steve Young tripped. But he regained his balance and threw over the middle of the field into the end zone.

The receiver he was targeting already had dropped four passes in the game against the Green Bay Packers. Plus he had lost a fumble. And three Packers now guarded him in the end zone. But that receiver was the talented Terrell Owens. And he caught the ball to give the 49ers the win.

"I was just happy that I caught the ball," Owens said. "I had a rough day. I let the team down in the beginning, but they all encouraged me to keep my head up."

Terrell Owens rose to stardom with the San Francisco 49ers in the late 1990s and early 2000s.

Owens loved the spotlight. He played with some of the NFL's most high-profile teams. And he caught 1,078 balls in his 15 pro seasons. Owens was strong, fast, and hard to tackle. That helped make him one of the NFL's most visible stars.

But Owens also made some enemies. As a 49er, he angered fans in Dallas by dancing on the Cowboys' midfield star. He later called his Philadelphia Eagles quarterback Donovan McNabb a quitter.

But there was no question about Owens's talent. He led the NFL in touchdown catches three times. He gained more than 1,000 yards through the air in nine seasons. And he was the Eagles' best player in their lone Super Bowl appearance, a loss to the New England Patriots in February 2005.

122

The number of receiving yards, on nine catches, for Owens in his only Super Bowl, coming off a broken leg that had sidelined him for a month in the 2004 season.

Terrell Owens runs into open space after making a catch for the Philadelphia Eagles in Super Bowl XXXIX.

TERRELL OWENS

Hometown: Alexander City, Alabama

College: University of Tennessee at Chattanooga

Height, Weight: 6-foot-3, 226 pounds

Birth Date: December 7, 1973

Teams: San Francisco 49ers (1996–2003)
Philadelphia Eagles (2004–05)
Dallas Cowboys (2006–08)
Buffalo Bills (2009)
Cincinnati Bengals (2010)

All-Pro: 2000, 2001, 2002, 2004, 2007

Pro Bowls: 2000, 2001, 2002, 2003, 2004, 2007

Super Bowl: XXXIX

TONY GONZALEZ

It was a simple 2-yard touchdown pass.
Hundreds of NFL players have caught one. But for Tony Gonzalez, it was special. The catch was his 100th NFL touchdown. Gonzalez became the only tight end in history with 100 touchdown catches. In fact, Gonzalez led tight ends in just about every receiving category through 2012.

"Tony, he kind of paved the way for me," said New Orleans Saints tight end Jimmy Graham, who played against Gonzalez's Atlanta Falcons that day.

Yet Gonzalez nearly didn't become a tight end in football. In college, he was an excellent basketball player. He often thought that would be his pro sport. But the Kansas City Chiefs took Gonzalez in the first round of the 1997 NFL Draft.

Tony Gonzalez developed a reputation as one of the NFL's best pass-catching tight ends while with the Kansas City Chiefs.

Gonzalez became a starter the next year. And he has been a star ever since. Gonzalez had the second-most catches in NFL history following the 2012 season.

Using his size, power, and unexpected speed, Gonzalez has done his best work over the middle. Receivers often get hit the most and the hardest in that area of the field. But he hasn't cared.

"Yeah, that's where I make my living," he said with a smile.

In 2004, Gonzalez became the first tight end to make 100 catches in a season. Four years earlier, he had gone over 1,000 yards receiving in one year. Gonzalez left the Chiefs and joined the Falcons in 2009. The team made the playoffs every season with him in the lineup through 2012.

1,242

The number of catches Gonzalez made in his career through 2012. He is the only tight end in pro football history to have more than 1,000 career catches through 2012.

Atlanta Falcons tight end Tony Gonzalez goes up for a catch against the Philadelphia Eagles in 2012.

TONY GONZALEZ

Hometown: Torrance, California

College: University of California, Berkeley

Height, Weight: 6-foot-5, 251 pounds

Birth Date: February 27, 1976

Teams: Kansas City Chiefs (1997–2008)
Atlanta Falcons (2009–)

All-Pro: 1999, 2000, 2001, 2003, 2008, 2012

Pro Bowls: 1999, 2000, 2001, 2002, 2003, 2004, 2005, 2006, 2007, 2008, 2010, 2011, 2012

RANDY MOSS

The New England Patriots needed a touchdown. So coach Bill Belichick told quarterback Tom Brady to throw the ball deep. They both knew Randy Moss would be there.

And he was. Moss sprinted past two New York Giants defenders. Then he caught the ball in stride and kept going. The 65-yard touchdown secured a 38–35 win. And that win made the 2007 Patriots the first team to finish a season 16–0.

The Giants ended the Patriots' unbeaten run in a Super Bowl rematch. Still, Moss had as great a season as any receiver. He made 98 catches for 1,493 yards. That was despite often being double- or even triple-teamed on most plays.

Randy Moss of the Minnesota Vikings rises above Atlanta Falcons defenders for a catch in 2003.

Moss was used to that, though. He led the NFL with 17 touchdown catches in his rookie season in 1998 with the Minnesota Vikings. That was the first of five times he led the league in scores. His best year, though, was that 2007 season with the Patriots.

23

The number of touchdown passes Moss caught, an NFL record, during the Patriots' 2007 unbeaten regular season.

Moss thrived using his speed and height. Few defensive backs were as fast as Moss. Fewer were even close to as tall. So Moss could provide a large target on short passes or for jump balls. He was at his best on deep balls, though. Moss could simply outrun most defenders.

Off-field problems sometimes overshadowed Moss's career. He played on five different teams. However, he settled down with the San Francisco 49ers in 2012. He helped the team reach Super Bowl XLVII after that season.

Randy Moss makes a one-handed catch for the New England Patriots in a 2010 game against the New York Jets.

RANDY MOSS

Hometown: Rand, West Virginia

College: Marshall University

Height, Weight: 6-foot-4, 215 pounds

Birth Date: February 13, 1977

Teams: Minnesota Vikings (1998–2004, 2010)
Oakland Raiders (2005–06)
New England Patriots (2007–10)
Tennessee Titans (2010)
San Francisco 49ers (2012)

All-Pro: 1998, 2000, 2003, 2007

Pro Bowls: 1998, 1999, 2000, 2002, 2003, 2007

Super Bowls: XLII, XLVII

REGGIE
WAYNE

Reggie Wayne was back in Miami, where he went to college. And his Indianapolis Colts were playing in Super Bowl XLI.

The opposing Chicago Bears jumped out to a 7–0 lead on the opening kickoff. Then Colts quarterback Peyton Manning was intercepted. But Wayne was ready when the Colts got the ball back. He broke free of the defense. Then Manning hit him for a 53-yard touchdown. That helped spark a 29–17 Colts victory in front of his friends and family.

"Greatest feeling in the world," Wayne said. "And to do it in my hometown . . . "

Reggie Wayne combined with Marvin Harrison to make a lethal pass-catching combo with the Indianapolis Colts.

The Colts drafted Wayne in 2001.
Through 2008, he teamed with Marvin Harrison to form the most dangerous receiving duo in football. But Harrison usually was Manning's top target in most of those years. It wasn't until 2007 that Wayne truly became the Colts' number one receiver. Wayne led the NFL with 1,510 yards that year. He caught 104 passes and scored 10 touchdowns.

Wayne had more than 1,000 receiving yards in eight of the nine seasons from 2004 to 2012. He fell just short in 2011. That year Manning was hurt and didn't play. Manning left the Colts before the 2012 season. Wayne could have followed him. But he instead stayed in Indianapolis and had one of his best seasons. He had 1,355 receiving yards. Plus he helped the Colts reach the playoffs just one year after the team had finished 2–14.

1,510

The number of receiving yards Wayne had in 2007, the most in the NFL and a career best. Wayne also caught 10 touchdown passes.

Reggie Wayne of the Indianapolis Colts dives for the football during a 2008 game against the Cincinnati Bengals.

REGGIE WAYNE

Hometown: New Orleans, Louisiana
College: University of Miami (Florida)
Height, Weight: 6-foot, 198 pounds
Birth Date: November 17, 1978
Team: Indianapolis Colts (2001–)
All-Pro: 2010
Pro Bowls: 2006, 2007, 2008, 2009, 2010, 2012
Super Bowls: XLI, XLIV

LARRY
FITZGERALD

Larry Fitzgerald broke free over the middle. Arizona Cardinals quarterback Kurt Warner spotted him. So Warner threaded a pass to Fitzgerald, who grabbed it between two Pittsburgh Steelers defenders. Off he went.

Fitzgerald ran all the way to the end zone for a 64-yard touchdown. Suddenly the underdog Cardinals led Super Bowl XLIII with less than three minutes remaining in the game.

Pittsburgh came back to win. But that play showed why Fitzgerald was considered one of the NFL's top receivers. He caught seven passes for 127 yards in the big game. His play nearly brought the Cardinals their first Super Bowl title.

Larry Fitzgerald of the Arizona Cardinals elevates above a Philadelphia Eagles defender for a catch in 2009.

Fitzgerald provides an easy target for quarterbacks. First, he is huge. He also is easy to spot with his long hair flowing out of his helmet. Fitzgerald is not, however, easy to stop. He is not afraid to run routes through the middle of the field. And with his large hands and long arms, he sucks in passes like a vacuum.

"If you throw it anywhere near him, he's going to get it," Warner said in 2009.

The Cardinals drafted Fitzgerald third overall in 2004. He caught 58 passes as a rookie. Then he soared to 103 catches in his second year to lead the NFL. Through 2012 he has had six seasons with more than 80 catches. Fitzgerald's Cardinals haven't always been successful. But defenders always know that big No. 11 will be ready to play at his best.

103

The number of catches Fitzgerald made in 2005, his second pro season. No Arizona Cardinals player has ever had more catches in one season through 2012.

Larry Fitzgerald reaches out for a catch for the Arizona Cardinals against the Seattle Seahawks in 2012.

LARRY FITZGERALD

Hometown: Minneapolis, Minnesota
College: University of Pittsburgh
Height, Weight: 6-foot-3, 225 pounds
Birth Date: August 31, 1983
Team: Arizona Cardinals (2004–)
All-Pro: 2008
Pro Bowls: 2005, 2007, 2008, 2009, 2010, 2011

CALVIN JOHNSON

"Megatron." It is a fearsome nickname for one of football's most dominating receivers.

Oddly, though, Calvin Johnson was not always a big-time pass catcher. He didn't break out until his final season in college at Georgia Tech. But he showed the Detroit Lions enough. They picked him second overall in the 2007 NFL Draft.

It was a smart move. Johnson has been a pass-catching machine for the Lions. In 2011, he helped them break an 11-season run of not making the playoffs. That year, Johnson led the NFL in receiving yards with 1,681. He shattered that mark the next year, gaining an NFL-record 1,964 receiving yards. Johnson also led the league with 122 catches.

Calvin Johnson is so big and so strong that few can stop the Detroit Lions' wide receiver.

Johnson leads a new wave of tall, fast, strong, and smart NFL receivers. He is a beast in the end zone. Defenders have little chance against him on jump balls. But Johnson also is known for his exact route running. He can burn defenders deep or short. If he's supposed to go eight steps and then cut inside, he does just that—not an inch farther.

"If I expect to catch the ball, I need to be where it is thrown," Johnson said of his route running.

Johnson is tough, too. He has played hurt in nearly every one of his pro seasons. So if he seems machine-like in the way he overpowers defenders or runs away from tacklers, well, what do they call him? Megatron!

17

The number of seasons that Jerry Rice held the record for most receiving yards (1,848) in a season. Johnson broke that record in 2012 with 1,964.

Calvin Johnson of the Detroit Lions uses his big body to get extra yards against the Indianapolis Colts in 2012.

CALVIN JOHNSON

Hometown: Tyrone, Georgia

College: Georgia Tech

Height, Weight: 6-foot-5, 239 pounds

Birth Date: September 25, 1985

Team: Detroit Lions (2007–)

All-Pro: 2011, 2012

Pro Bowls: 2010, 2011, 2012

HONORABLE MENTIONS

Tim Brown – Brown, who also was a fine punt returner, made more than 1,000 catches for the Los Angeles and Oakland Raiders, mostly during the 1990s.

Mike Ditka – The NFL's first great all-around tight end, Ditka was a strong blocker and steady receiver for the 1960s Chicago Bears.

Tom Fears – The former defensive back switched to offense for the 1940s and 1950s Los Angeles Rams, and he once caught 18 passes in a game.

Charlie Joiner – He played 239 games in 18 seasons, which was more games than any other receiver when he retired in 1986.

John Mackey – One of the first fast tight ends, Mackey caught six touchdown passes of more than 50 yards in 1966 for the Baltimore Colts.

John Stallworth – He won four Super Bowls with the Pittsburgh Steelers during the 1970s.

Lynn Swann – The Steelers' wide receiver made dozens of leaping and diving catches and was MVP of Super Bowl X after the 1975 season.

Lionel Taylor – He led the AFL five times in receptions and averaged more than 100 yards per game in 1960 while with the Denver Broncos.

Wes Welker – He made more than 100 catches in five seasons from 2007 to 2012, which was a key to the high-scoring New England Patriots offense.

GLOSSARY

All-America
An honor given to the top athletes in college sports.

draft
A system used by professional sports leagues to select new players in order to spread incoming talent among all teams. The NFL Draft is held each April.

playoffs
A series of single-elimination games after the regular season that determine which two teams meet in the Super Bowl.

Pro Bowl
An annual All-Star game that takes place one week before the Super Bowl.

rookie
A first-year player in the NFL.

routes
The paths in which receivers are supposed to run in a given football play.

FOR MORE INFORMATION

Further Readings

Gramling, Gary. *Sports Illustrated Kids 1st and 10: Top 10 Lists of Everything in Football*. New York: Sports Illustrated, 2011.

Guess McKerley, Jennifer. *Science Behind Sports: Football*. Farmington Hills, MI: Lucent Books, 2011.

Web Links

To learn more about the NFL's best receivers, visit ABDO Publishing Company online at **www.abdopublishing.com**. Web sites about the NFL's best receivers are featured on our Book Links page. These links are routinely monitored and updated to provide the most current information available.

INDEX

Alworth, Lance, 14–17
American Football League (AFL), 14–16, 17
Arizona Cardinals, 54–56, 57
Atlanta Falcons, 42–44, 45

Baltimore Colts, 10–12, 13
Belichick, Bill, 46
Berry, Raymond, 10–13
Buffalo Bills, 41

Carter, Cris, 30–33
Chicago Bears, 50
Cincinnati Bengals, 41
Cleveland Browns, 18–20, 21

Dallas Cowboys, 16, 17, 40, 41
Detroit Lions, 8, 58, 61

Fitzgerald, Larry, 54–57

Gonzalez, Tony, 42–45
Green Bay Packers, 6–8, 9, 38

Hall of Fame, 8, 12, 16, 20, 24, 28, 32
Harrison, Marvin, 34–37, 52
Houston Oilers, 22–24
Hutson, Don, 6–9

Indianapolis Colts, 34–36, 37, 50–52, 53

Johnson, Calvin, 58–61

Kansas City Chiefs, 42–44, 45

Largent, Steve, 8, 22–25

Miami Dolphins, 20, 21, 33
Minnesota Vikings, 30–32, 33, 48, 49
Moss, Randy, 28, 32, 46–49

New England Patriots, 40, 46–48, 49
New Orleans Saints, 42
New York Giants, 10, 46
NFL Draft, 18, 42, 52, 56, 58
NFL MVP Award, 8

Oakland Raiders, 14, 29, 49
Owens, Terrell, 38–41

Philadelphia Eagles, 33, 40, 41
Pittsburgh Steelers, 54

Rice, Jerry, 24, 26–29, 32, 36, 60

San Diego Chargers, 14–16, 17
San Francisco 49ers, 26–28, 29, 38–40, 41, 48, 49
Seattle Seahawks, 22–24, 25, 29
Shula, Don, 20

Tennessee Titans, 49

Walsh, Bill, 28
Warfield, Paul, 18–21
Wayne, Reggie, 50–53

ABOUT THE AUTHOR

Barry Wilner has been a sportswriter for the Associated Press since 1976. He has written about every sport and has covered every Super Bowl since 1985. He also has covered the World Cup, the Stanley Cup Finals, the Summer and Winter Olympics, the Pan American Games, championship boxing matches, major golf and tennis tournaments, and auto races.